S0-BBN-587

Leni Donlan

Chicago, Illinois

Published by Raintree,
A division of Reed Elsevier Inc.
Chicago, Illinois

Customer Service: **888-454-2279**

Visit our website at **www.raintreelibrary.com**

Designed by Kimberly R. Miracle and Betsy Wernert
Photo Research by Tracy Cummins
Maps on pages 16 and 29 by Mapping Specialists
Printed in China by Leo Paper Group

12 11 10 09 08
10 9 8 7 6 5 4 3 2 1

Library of Congress Cataloging-in-Publication Data
Donlan, Leni.
Working for change : the struggle for women's rights / Leni Donlan. -- 1st ed.
p. cm. -- (American history through primary sources)
Includes bibliographical references and index.
ISBN 978-1-4109-2700-2 (hc) -- ISBN 978-1-4109-2711-8 (pb)
1. Women--Suffrage--United States--Juvenile literature. I. Title.
JK1898.D66 2008
324.6'230973--dc22

2007005912

Acknowledgments
The author and publisher are grateful to the following for permission to reproduce copyright material:Library of Congress Rare Book and Special Collections Division **pp. 4, 25, 27**; Library of Congress Prints and Photographs Division **pp. 5, 6, 9 (left), 9 (right), 10, 12, 15, 16, 17, 18, 19, 21, 22, 23, 24, 26, 28, 29 (bottom)**; Library of Congress Geography and Map Division **p. 8**; Nebraska State Historical Society Photograph collections **p. 13**.

Cover image of a Suffrage parade, New York City, May 6, 1912, reproduced with permission of the Library of Congress Prints and Photographs Division.

The publishers would like to thank Nancy Harris for her assistance in the preparation of this book.

Contents

Some words are printed in bold, **like this**. You can find out what they mean on page 30. You can also look in the box at the bottom of the page where they first appear.

Remember the Ladies

July 4, 1776, was an important day. The **Declaration of Independence** was signed. This paper said that the United States wanted to be a new country. It no longer wanted to be ruled by the country of England. It would decide what laws and freedoms its people would have.

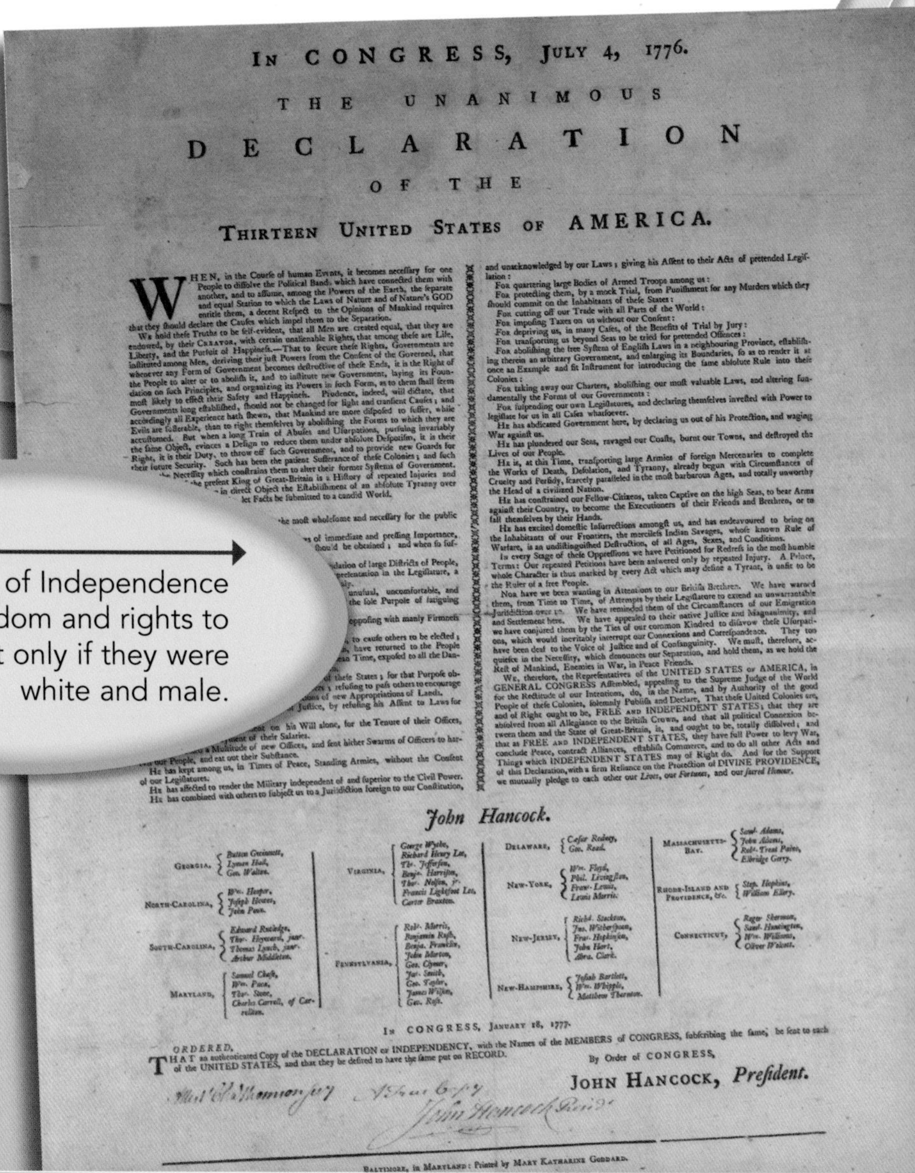
IN CONGRESS, JULY 4, 1776.

THE UNANIMOUS

DECLARATION

OF THE

THIRTEEN UNITED STATES OF AMERICA.

John Hancock.

IN CONGRESS, JANUARY 18, 1777.

ORDERED,

THAT an authenticated Copy of the DECLARATION OF INDEPENDENCY, with the Names of the MEMBERS of CONGRESS, subscribing the same, be sent to each of the UNITED STATES, and that they be desired to have the same put on RECORD.

By Order of CONGRESS,

JOHN HANCOCK, *President.*

The Declaration of Independence offered freedom and rights to Americans. But only if they were white and male.

ancestor person who lived before you

Declaration of Independence writing sent to the king of England. It said Americans would no longer be ruled by England.

Abigail Adams asked her husband to work toward equal rights for men and women.

John Adams helped write the Declaration of Independence. He later became the second president of the United States. Abigail Adams was John's wife. She wanted women to have the same rights as men. Rights are feedoms. Being able to vote is a right.

Abigail told John: "Remember the Ladies, and be more generous and **favorable** [helpful] to them than your **ancestors** [the people who lived before you]." Abigail meant that women did not have equal rights in the past. She wanted John to work toward giving women equal rights in the future.

Sadly, the men who planned the new nation did not "remember the ladies." It took years for this to happen.

A Woman's Place

NOTICE.

I HEREBY forewarn all persons against crediting my wife, DELILAH McCONNELL, on my account, as she has absconded without my consent. I am therefore determined to pay none of her contracts.

WILLIAM McCONNELL. 13—2

May 15, 1828.

ᎢᏣᏍᎬᎦ.

ᎠᏂ ᏃᏉ ᏥᏁᎩ, ᏂᎦᏍ ᏴᏫ ᎢᏣᏍᏁᏗ. Ꮃ
ᏍᏗ ᎩᏣ ᏜᏅᏓᏁᏍᏗ ᎠᏴ ᎠᏆᎫᏴᏗ ᎨᏒᎢ, ᎠᏆᏢ
ᎨᎢ ᏗᏔᎸ ᏧᏁᎢᏍ. ᎠᏉᎯᏳᏅᏋᏃ ᏂᎨᏒᎾ ᎠᏆ
ᎨᏗᏒᏭ. ᏣᏍᎩᏂ ᎠᏆᎫᏴᏗ ᏜᎩ, ᏃᏉ ᏥᏁᎩ
ᎠᏴ ᎠᏆᎫᏴᏗ ᏅᏋᏭᏒ ᏔᏥᏓᏂᏁᏯᎢ.

ᎾᎨ ᏅᎩᏏᏅᏗ.

ᏍᎩᎦᏓᏏᏁ ᎢᎦ ᎠᏅᏍᎬᏗ, 1828.

decision choice
property something owned, like land or a home

In the early 1800s, women did not have many rights. They were told what they could or could not do. Sometimes, churches told them this. The United States government (leaders) also told them what to do.

Women could not vote. This means they could not choose the leaders of the country. They could not hold a job in the government. Women could not go to schools or colleges. Married women could not own a home. Women could not leave their husbands.

Most people believed that men and women had their own "place." A woman's place was in the home. She should cook and clean. She should raise the children. It was a man's place to make **decisions**. The man made the choices for his family. He also made decisions about his business and **property**. Property is what a person owns. Only men made decisions about the laws (rules) of the country.

Many women wanted to make important decisions, too. Women began working to change things. Women wanted the right to vote. They thought that this would change things.

In the 1800s, men were in charge of their wives. A man wrote this note. It told people not to sell anything to his wife. This was because she had left him.

Seneca Falls Convention

In July of 1848, some women were talking. Two of the women were Elizabeth Cady Stanton and Lucretia Mott. The women talked about women's rights. They wanted more people to think and talk about women's rights. They decided to hold a **convention**. This is a large meeting. That way, many people could discuss the rights of women.

Stanton wrote a paper for the convention. It was called the **Declaration of Sentiments**. It explained the rights women should have. Her paper was like the **Declaration of Independence**. But it said "all men *and women* are created equal."

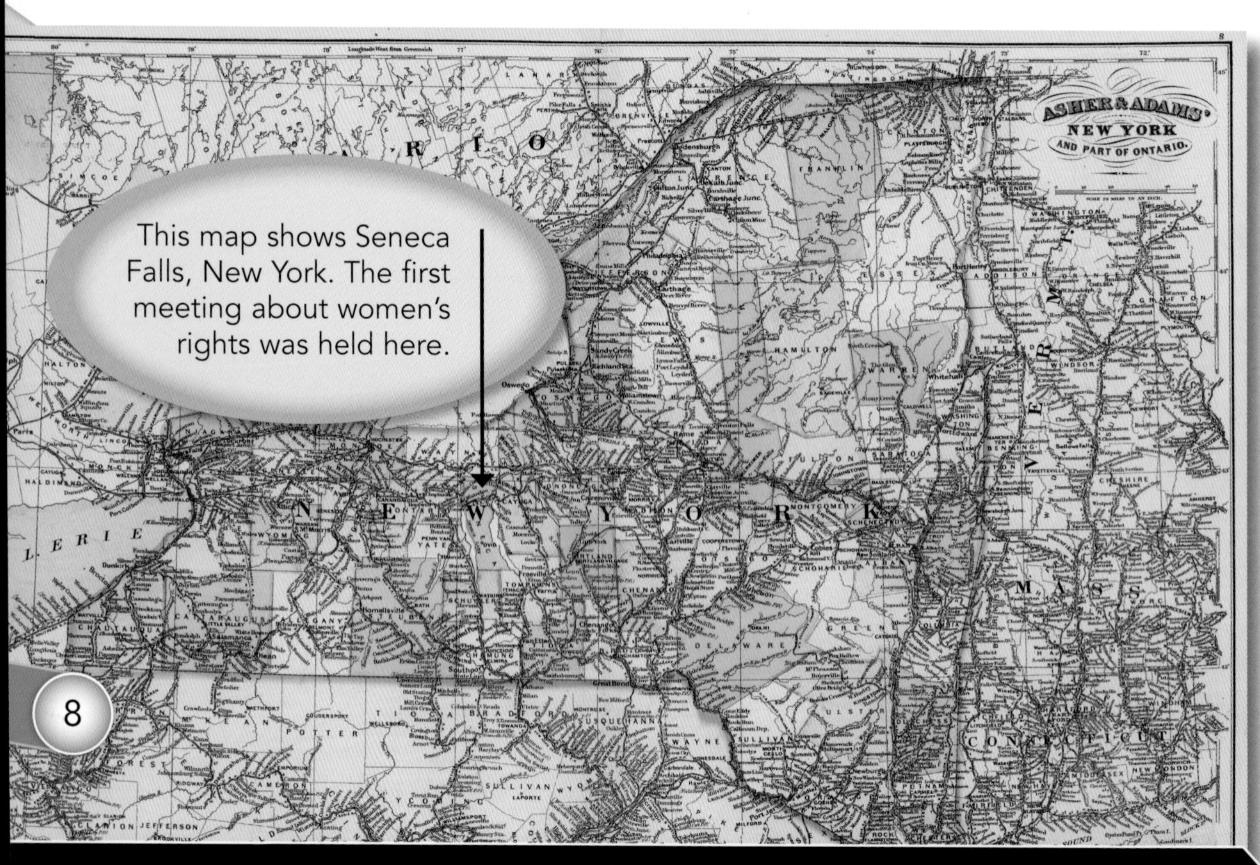

This map shows Seneca Falls, New York. The first meeting about women's rights was held here.

convention large meeting
Declaration of Sentiments writing that said what rights women should have
resolution written idea of what should happen

Elizabeth Cady Stanton and Lucretia Mott worked together for many years They worked for women's rights.

Stanton also wrote eleven **resolutions**. A resolution is an idea for what should happen. The ninth resolution was shocking for this time. It said women should have the right to vote! They wanted to help choose their leaders.

The convention was held in Stanton's hometown. She was from Seneca Falls, New York (see map). Not many people were expected to be there.

Frederick Douglass wanted rights for all people. It did not matter if they were black or white. It did not matter if they were men or women.

progress movement toward a goal
slave person who is owned by another person
suffrage right to vote

A good start

About 300 people attended the **convention**! That was far more than expected.

Frederick Douglass was at the convention. He was one of 40 men to attend it. Douglass had been a **slave**. He used to be owned. He had no rights. Now, he worked for a newspaper. He was well respected. Douglass spoke up about the ninth **resolution**. He believed in women's **suffrage**. Suffrage is the right to vote. He was able to talk the convention into passing the ninth resolution.

Later, many people made fun of the convention. They also made fun of the its resolutions. Stanton felt the attention was good. She said: "It will start women thinking, and men too; and when men and women think about a new question, the first step in **progress** [movement toward a goal] is taken."

A long time to wait

Charlotte Woodward attended the Seneca Falls Convention. She was one of the youngest people to attend. She was a very old woman when she was finally able to vote. This was 72 years after the convention had been held. She was the only one who lived long enough to vote.

Women Work for Change

Women worked to get equal rights. Slowly, they made **progress**. They slowly got closer to their goal.

Women worked for education rights. In 1821 Emma Hart Willard opened one of the first school for girls. Colleges for women also opened. Two of these were Mount Holyoke and Vassar. Then, colleges began to allow both men and women to attend. Oberlin was one of the first colleges to do this. (See the map on page 29.)

Vassar College was one of the first colleges for women.

This is a photo of the Chrisman sisters. They claimed this property in Nebraska through the Homestead Act of 1862.

Homesteaders

The U.S. Homestead Act of 1862 allowed men *and* women to get free public land. People 21 years or older could claim land. They had to build a home. They had to live there and farm the land. After five years, they would own the land.

Women started to have other rights. In Connecticut women were allowed to write **wills**. They could decide who got their belongings after they died. In 1839 Mississippi allowed women to own **property**. Mississippi women could now own land and homes.

In 1848 New York gave women property rights. California did the same in 1849.

Sojourner Truth

In the mid-1800s, many people worked to end **slavery**. Slavery was the practice of owning people. These people were called **abolitionists**. Sojourner Truth had been a slave. She became an abolitionist. She helped other slaves become free. Truth also supported equal rights for women.

Truth gave a famous speech at a women's **convention**. The meeting was in 1851. The speech was called "Ain't I a Woman?" Other speakers spoke against women and blacks. They said they did not need the same rights as white men. Truth did not agree. She explained that it was a problem. She said this because so many people kept talking about these rights. She said that people should listen to what women had to say.

Strong words

Sojourner Truth was six feet tall. She had a deep voice. When she spoke, people usually listened. Truth said this in her "Ain't I a Woman?" speech: "And now they [women] is asking to do it [vote], the men better let them."

Sojourner Truth was an excellent speaker. She helped convince people that women and black men should have rights. They should have the same rights as white men.

abolitionist person who worked to stop slavery
slavery practice of owning people

Civil War

A **civil war** is a war between people who live in the same country. From 1861 to 1865 there was a civil war in the United States. The Northern and Southern states fought each other. Many people died in the U.S. Civil War. The war finally put an end to **slavery**. People could no longer be owned.

Elizabeth Cady Stanton (left) and Susan B. Anthony (right) were good friends.

During the Civil War, husbands were away fighting the war. Women had to do their jobs. Women had to make **decisions** (choices) on their own. When the war ended, women were stronger than ever.

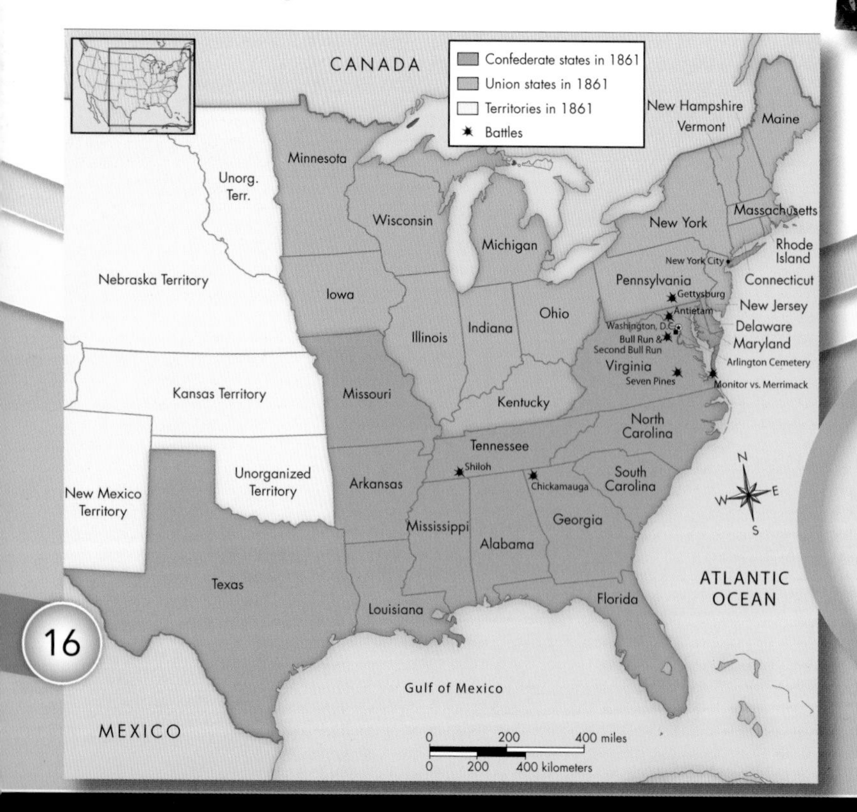

This map shows the United States during the Civil War. The Union states were in the North. The Confederate states were in the South.

civil war war between two groups of people who live in the same country

Men and women worked together to help soldiers during the U.S. Civil War.

In 1866 two friends started a new national **organization**. The two friends were Elizabeth Cady Stanton and Susan B. Anthony. An organization is a group that works together for a purpose. The group was called the American Equal Rights Association (AERA). The AERA wanted equal rights for women.

The AERA held a **convention** (meeting) in New York City. The year was 1867. The AERA started working on rights for everyone. They worked on **suffrage**, the right to vote, for everyone.

Government Changes

After the **Civil War**, **slaves** were freed. They were no longer owned. Most slaves were black. Black men now had rights. They could vote.

Most women were glad that slavery was **abolished** (ended). They were glad that black men could vote. But they were sad that women did not get **suffrage**.

In 1872 women did not have the right to vote. Still, hundreds of women planned to vote anyway. Many women were stopped at the **polls**. These are places where people vote. But some women, like Susan B. Anthony, did vote. A few weeks later, Anthony was arrested for voting. She had broken the law, or rule, against women voting.

1280

AN
ACCOUNT OF THE PROCEEDINGS
ON THE
TRIAL OF
SUSAN B. ANTHONY,
ON THE
Charge of Illegal Voting,
AT THE
PRESIDENTIAL ELECTION IN NOV., 1872,
AND ON THE
TRIAL OF
BEVERLY W. JONES, EDWIN T. MARSH
AND WILLIAM B. HALL,
THE INSPECTORS OF ELECTION BY WHOM HER VOTE WAS RECEIVED.

ROCHESTER, N. Y.:
DAILY DEMOCRAT AND CHRONICLE BOOK PRINT, 3 WEST MAIN ST.
1874.

When Susan B. Anthony voted in 1872, this was a crime. Her case got a lot of public attention. Would a case about voting get public attention today?

abolish get rid of; do away with
poll place where voting takes place

This is a photo of Susan B. Anthony. She was sure that women would some day get the right to vote.

Not a word

After the U.S. Civil War ended, Sojourner Truth said: "There is a great stir about colored men getting their rights, but not a word about... women." She meant that people were talking about black men being able to vote. But no one was talking about women's rights.

Change Continues

Women continued to work for human rights. Sometimes women and children are hurt by a family member. This is called **domestic violence**. In 1874 the Woman's Christian Temperance Union (WCTU) was formed. The group wanted women and children to be safe at home. They wanted them safe from domestic violence.

The WCTU had strong leaders. Annie Turner Wittenmyer helped start the WCTU. She was the first president of the group. Frances Willard became the second president in 1879.

Through the WCTU, Willard helped women get **organized** to fight for change. They were ready to act. She helped women become leaders. The WCTU was very important for women's **suffrage** or right to vote. It was also important for making other changes.

Frances Willard was well educated. She was a good writer and speaker. She made a wonderful leader of the WCTU.

Out West

In the 1800s, life was hard in the western United States. It was hard for all people. But women there got more respect than in the East. Women could own **property** in the West. Women also ran businesses. These things made people think. They saw that women should have the same rights as men.

In 1869 Wyoming Territory allowed women to vote. (Wyoming was not a state yet.) In 1893 Colorado was the first state to allow women to vote. Soon after, Utah, Idaho, and Washington gave women the right to vote.

Life out West was hard. But women were treated more fairly here.

defeat not allowed; does not win

This cartoon shows a woman walking from the West to the East. Women in the West were able to vote before women in the East. The states that allowed suffrage are labeled. So are the territories.

Susan B. Anthony and other women's **suffrage** leaders traveled to California. They helped Californian women fight for their right to vote. They helped them fight for other rights, too. Women's suffrage was **defeated** (not allowed) twice in California. This happened in 1896 and in 1906. But it passed in 1911!

Kansas, Oregon, and Arizona allowed suffrage in 1912. Alaska Territory allowed suffrage in 1913. (Alaska was not a state yet.) Montana and Nevada gave women the right to vote in 1914.

Women Make More Progress

In the early 1900s, big cities had many problems. There were poor working conditions. There was also low pay for workers. Men and women worked very long hours. Even children worked long hours! Women went on **strike**. They stopped working until conditions got better. Women helped get laws passed to **protect** workers. These laws helped keep workers safe.

Women also worked to change living conditions in cities. They worked to improve **sanitation**. Sanitation services keep cities clean.

These women are on strike. They are against long hours and unsafe conditions at work.

SOCIETY WOMEN NOW JOIN IN SUFFRAGETTE PROPAGANDA

Prominent Names of List of Those Who Will Attend To-Day's Rally.

THE "ANTIS" ALSO PLAN AN OPPOSITION MEETING

One Gathering in Carnegie Hall and the Other in Berkeley Lyceum.

What will be the most important meeting for the cause of suffrage ever held in this country will take place this afternoon in Carnegie Hall, and a number of prominent women who have heretofore had nothing to do with the propaganda will be among those present. Every seat in the hall will be taken. The choice ones were engaged more than a month ago. There will also be a number of men prominent in business and in the professions in the audience, and several speeches will be made by men who favor giving women the right to vote.

While this meeting is going on there is also to be another in Berkeley Lyceum, where those who are opposed to the suffrage movement will hold forth. Both men and women who are against giving women the franchise will speak, and messengers will be kept busy going between the hostile camps to report how the other meeting is progressing.

It is expected, however, that the meeting at Carnegie Hall will be the larger one, and no mention will be made there of there being any other.

Mrs. Philip Snowden, wife of a member of the English Parliament, will address the Carnegie Hall meeting. Rabbi Stephen S. Wise will be another speaker. The Rev. Dr. Aked, pastor of the Fifth Avenue Baptist Church, and Mrs. Carrie Chapman Catt, president of the Interurban Council of Woman Suffrage League, will be the other speakers. Mrs. Catt will preside and make the closing address.

Among those who will occupy the first tier of boxes are Mrs. Clarence Mackay, Mrs. George J. Gould, Mrs. Ernesto Fabbri, Mrs. Robert Goelet, Mrs. Henry Miller, Richard Stevens, Oliver Iselin, Mrs. Philip Lydig, Mrs. John Pratt, Mrs. Egerton Winthrop, Jr.; Mrs. William K. Vanderbilt, Jr.; Miss Dorothy Whitney, Mrs. Perry Belmont and Miss Anne Fitzhugh Miller, of Geneva, N. Y.

Among those who will occupy seats on the platform are William M. Ivins, Charles Sprague Smith, Professor John Devey, Mrs. Bourke Cockran and Mrs. Richard Aldrich.

The Interurban Woman Suffrage Council, under whose auspices the meeting is to be held, includes eighteen suffrage leagues in Manhattan and Bronx, whose membe… will be represented in the audience. … the other woman suffrage organizations … the city will be present.

"Woman suffrage is on its way," said Miss Hay, "and it doesn't look as if it would be very long in coming, either. Those who have watched the suffrage movement have predicted that it would finally come, as it seems to be doing, in a rush that is almost overwhelming."

At the meeting of the Interurban Coun-

MRS. PHILIP M. LYDIG
PHOTO. BY HISTED.

SOCIETY WOM…

Women continued to have meetings to talk about equal rights. Many very wealthy and popular women attended this meeting.

Over time, more women worked outside the home. Women who studied in college had important jobs. They were lawyers and doctors. They were teachers.

Women planned meetings and parades. They did this to get attention for women's **suffrage** (right to vote). More and more women became involved.

More men began to think women should be allowed to vote.

Woman Suffrage—Finally!

In the early 1900s, older leaders were tired from the long struggle. Younger women began to lead the work.

The U.S. government considered a women's **suffrage amendment**. The year was 1918. An amendment is a change to a law (rule). President Woodrow Wilson gave his support for women's right to vote. He lead the country at this time. The woman suffrage amendment finally passed on August 26, 1920.

This card was given out at the National American Woman's Suffrage Association event. This event was held in Washington, D.C.

amendment change to a law
mosaic art that uses small pieces of colored stone or glass to make a picture
victory win

Never give up

This is a photo of Susan B. Anthony. She was very important in the fight for suffrage. Another suffrage worker said this about her:

"She never knew **defeat**.... She never doubted that **victory** (winning) was just ahead."

Women fought for more than 100 years. Finally, all women in the United States could vote.

Alice Paul was one of the leaders for women's suffrage in 1918. She said: "Each of us puts in one little stone, and then you get a great **mosaic** at the end." A mosaic is a picture made of many smaller pictures. She meant that thousands of women worked for suffrage. They worked in different ways. They worked at different times.

Museum of Suffrage

By 1900 women's **suffrage** seemed possible. More and more women (and men) were working to make it happen. Here are more pictures of the struggle.

These women were serious! They wanted the vote. This parade took place in New York City on May 6, 1912.

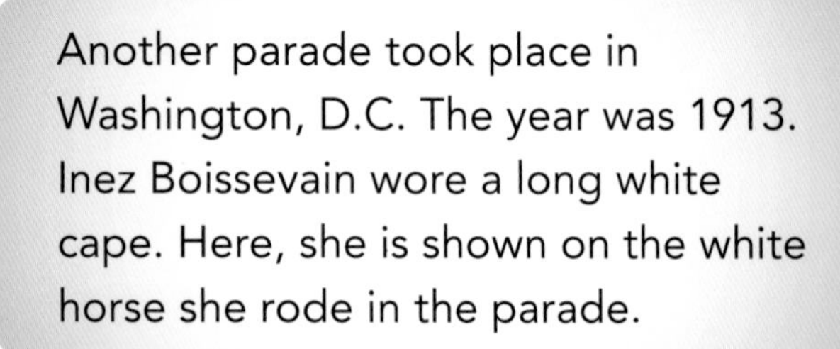

Another parade took place in Washington, D.C. The year was 1913. Inez Boissevain wore a long white cape. Here, she is shown on the white horse she rode in the parade.

In 1917 women got the vote in New York. These women were voting for the first time! How do you think they might have felt?

All of the places mentioned in the book can be found on this map.

Women could vote in New York and other states. But in 1917, they still could not vote in every state. These young women are holding signs in front of the White House. The president lives there. They wanted to let President Wilson know how they felt. They wanted him to change the laws (rules) so that all women could vote.

Glossary

abolish get rid of; do away with

abolitionist person who worked to stop slavery

amendment change to a law

ancestor person who lived before you

civil war war between two groups of people who live in the same country

convention large meeting

decision choice

Declaration of Independence writing sent to the king of England, in which Americans said they would no longer be ruled by England

Declaration of Sentiments writing that said what rights women should have

defeat not allowed; does not win

domestic violence crimes against family members that happen in the home

favorable another way to say "helpful"

mosaic art that uses small pieces of colored stone or glass to make a picture

organization group of people who work together for a purpose

organize be in order; be ready to act

poll place where voting takes place

progress movement toward a goal

property something owned, like land or a home

protect keep safe

resolution written idea of what should happen

sanitation methods of caring for public health, such as trash removal

slave person who is owned by another

slavery practice of owning people

society group of people who have common interests, beliefs, and purposes

strike stop work and carry signs to get attention; used when changes in the workplace are needed

suffrage right to vote

victory win

will what should happen to your property after you die

Want to Know More?

Books to read

- Corey, Shana. *You Forgot Your Skirt, Amelia Bloomer*. New York: Scholastic, 2000.
- Fritz, Jean. *You Want Women to Vote, Lizzie Stanton?* New York: Putnam's, 1995.
- McCully, Emily Arnold. *The Ballot Box Battle*. New York: Knopf, 1996.
- Sullivan, George. *The Day the Women Got the Vote: A Photo History of the Women's Rights Movement*. New York: Scholastic, 1994.

Websites

- **Political Culture and Imagery of American Woman Suffrage**
  http://www.nmwh.org/exhibits/intro.html
  Read more about women's suffrage and visit the picture gallery created on the National Museum of Women's History website.
- **Western New York Suffragists: Winning the Vote**
  http://winningthevote.org *Learn more about how women won the vote.*
- **The Second Day of the Seneca Falls Convention, July 20, 1848**
  http://www.americaslibrary.gov/cgi-bin/page.cgi/jb/reform/seneca_1
  Learn more about the Seneca Falls Convention on this website from the Library of Congress.

Places to visit

- **The National Women's Hall of Fame**
  76 Fall Street, Seneca Falls, NY 13148, (313) 568-8060 greatwomen.org

Read **When Will I Get In?: Segregation and Civil Rights** to find out about the struggle against segregation and Jim Crow laws.

Index